Closing the Gap

The Journey of a Peacemaker

_____
name

_____
date

Copyright © 2020 by Cheryl Miller and Quantum Circles Press

Scripture quotations are taken from the Holy Bible, New Living Translation, copyright ©1996, 2004, 2007, 2013, 2015 by Tyndale House Foundation. Used by permission of Tyndale House Publishers, Inc., Carol Stream, Illinois 60188. All rights reserved.

All rights reserved. No part of this book may be reproduced in any form or by any means, including photocopying, recording, or other electronic or mechanical methods without the prior written permission from the publisher.

Printed in the United States of America

ISBN 978-0-9859546-4-2

Quantum Circles Press

Some yearn to make a difference in the world.

Some have hearts that ache hoping to bring peace into the chaos that is sadly far too common in our daily human interactions.

If you are one such peacemaker, welcome!

This journey is designed to help you search out your calling.

This journey is designed to provide opportunities to see the world through different lenses.

This journey is one that requires diligence, unabashed hope, and at times quiet rest.

We hope the words on this page encourage, instruct, and lead you deeper in your journey as a peacemaker.

Contents

About the Cover Photo

Types of Prayer

Week 1 - Sin

Week 2 - Truth

Week 3 - Repentance

Week 4 - Forgiveness

Week 5 - Reconciliation

Week 6 - Justice

Week 7 - Love

About the Cover Photo

The photo on the cover was taken by the author during a reconciliation pilgrimage to the Middle East. If you look closely, you will see a structure built into the side of the cliff. That building is the Monastery of Saints John and George of Choziba, a cliff-hanging complex carved into sheer rock. It overlooks an unexpectedly lush garden with olive and cypress trees.

The setting is in a deep and narrow gorge called Wadi Qelt. The Wadi winds its deep and tortuous course between Jerusalem and Jericho.

In Biblical times the road from Jerusalem to Jericho was notorious for its danger and difficulty. It was known as the "Way of Blood" because of the blood which is often shed there by robbers." It wound its way through the canyon with turns and twists among the rocks creating places for criminals and robbers to hide then surprise passersby. Wadi Qelt is the road on which Jesus set the parable of the Good Samaritan (Luke 10:25-37). Some believe it is what inspired the writing of the 23rd Psalm and the "valley of the shadow of death."

A place that is notorious for sin, crime, and danger is also the place where we are reassured even in the dark places our God comforts us. And Christ brings it to the light as he uses this stark setting to illustrate the power of loving our neighbor.

In this journal, there are different types of prayer and reflections used as the method to pray each day.

Day 1 – Centering Prayer

Day 2 – Read and Reflect

Day 3 – Prayer of Lament

Day 4 – Intercessory Prayer

Day 5 – Prayer of Thanksgiving

Day 6 – Lectio Divina

Day 7 – A Concluding Prayer

Each week begins with one of seven topics:
SIN ~ TRUTH ~ REPENTANCE ~ FORGIVENESS
RECONCILIATION ~ JUSTICE ~ LOVE

Scripture is integral in understanding our journey as a peacemaker. It is also a roadmap and can become an example of how to pray. Use the scripture included each week as a focal point as you engage the different methods of prayer. Each day you will have opportunity to share your heart and burdens with your loving Father. And each day you will have opportunity to hear and journal his heart in response. Finally, the week will end with a prayer of conclusion based on the theme that week.

After working with victims and offenders of violent crime for years, it became evident there was a journey toward the peace that is found when the process works. As a volunteer mediator for the Victim/Offender Mediation Dialogue program (VOMD), I saw this process play out over and over. Each case was the same. It started with sin, whether it was greed, lust, anger, sin was impetus for the crime. Once the mediation process began we would wade through each of the topics covered in this prayer journal.

These topics mark out the path of peacemaking. All harm, conflict, injustice, and crime have the same starting point, sin. Even in cases where harm was not done intentionally, there is the reality of thoughtlessness and not thinking of and considering others before ourselves. To initiate the peacemaking process, we must address the sin for what it is.

This leads to truth. The one who sins needs to take responsibility for the harm done to another. Truth needs to be acknowledged by all impacted by the sin. The offender must accept and own the full impact of the harm done. The victim, or person hurt, is given the opportunity to speak truth about how the actions of the offender have impacted their life. Once truth is spoken, repentance should emerge.

Repentance must follow truth for the offender to know and understand all that needs to be confessed and repented. Unfortunately, there are many times where the offender will not acknowledge truth and repent. When there is no repentance the journey toward peacemaking is halted, or at the very least delayed. **The person harmed can still move to the next phase and forgive, but it is unlikely reconciliation can occur. In minor disputes, conflicting individuals can** choose to forgive even where there is no repentance—choosing to "agree to disagree" and putting aside the issue to salvage a relationship. But when the harm is significant, moving toward reconciliation without truth and the repentance of the offender can be dangerous. At the very least, it has great potential for ongoing or future harm.

However, when there is acknowledgment of sin, truth spoken of the harm and impact, with repentance by the offender, then forgiveness should follow. Forgiveness is the gift we all want to receive, but hold tight to the chest when required to give. Like repentance, it is challenging to move forward in peacemaking and reconciliation where forgiveness is not granted. In extreme cases where there is significant harm and trauma, forgiveness may take more effort.

Making it past forgiveness allows for all involved to be reconciled. And when reconciliation occurs, justice can be ushered in. When justice rolls down, love follows. Love does not always mean the one harmed will feel love toward the one who did the harm, though that does happen. This also manifests for the one harmed by feeling loved that someone spent the time and energy listening to their truth, joining in the sorrow, and walking along side. Yes, peacemakers, walking friends and families through challenging circumstances is a wonderful opportunity to show love to those who are hurting.

So, as you move through the weeks ahead, consider this journey. This journal will challenge you to think of times you have been hurt, times you have hurt others, and injustices around you that have caused great harm. As you reflect on these times, consider where the process is on this spectrum. Then start at the beginning and look honestly at the sin to allow you to move toward love. In the final week, poerty is used to reflect the theme.

CENTERING PRAYER

Be still, and know that I am God! I will be honored by every nation.
I will be honored throughout the world.
Psalm 46:10

Centering prayer is a method of silent prayer in which we experience God's immanent presence with us. It is grounded in relationship with God, through Christ, with a goal to both practice and nurture that relationship. It offers a way to grow in intimacy with God, moving beyond conversation to communion. The focus of centering prayer is the deepening of our relationship with the living Christ.

Steps for Centering Prayer

1. Set a timer. If you are new to centering prayer start with five minutes. You can always increase the time as you learn to remain in his presence.
2. Sit still, close your eyes, and begin to quiet yourself.
3. Choose a sacred word. It can be a word that focuses on an attribute of God or the name of God.
4. Allow yourself to focus on being present with the Triune God: the Father, Jesus, and the Holy Spirit.
5. The purpose is simply to be in the presence of the Holy One.
6. When thoughts or disruptions enter your mind, think of your sacred word to remind and center you back in the sweet presence of God.

PRAYER OF LAMENT

They went to the olive grove called Gethsemane, and Jesus said, "Sit here while I go and pray." He took Peter, James, and John with him, and he became deeply troubled and distressed. He told them, "My soul is crushed with grief to the point of death. Stay here and keep watch with me." He went on a little farther and fell to the ground. He prayed that, if it were possible, the awful hour awaiting him might pass him by.

Mark 14:32-35

We can worship God and pray to him during times we are in the midst of difficulty, suffering, or sorrow. It can be our sorrow and the struggles of others that move us to prayers of lament. So many individuals in the Bible poured their hearts out to God in lament. Jesus modeled this for us in Mark. When experiencing the dark night of the soul, prayers of lament are powerful. As you move through the weeks in this prayer journey, be sure to focus one day each week on a prayer of lament either inspired by the passages that week or the circumstances the scriptures reference.

Tips for a prayer of lament.

1. If it is your sorrow and suffering that come to mind, allow yourself to fully experience the emotions involved. From that place of pain, speak to God. Tell him your heart and thoughts of the sorrow or suffering. Ask him to be with you in the dark places. Praise him in spite of the situation.
2. If it is the sorrow and suffering of others that come to mind, ask God to show you his heart for those in their suffering. Again, allow yourself to feel any emotions that arise from that request. Ask God to comfort those in suffering. And finally, ask God how you can be a support or help others in times of distress and sorrow.
3. Use scriptures of lament as an inspiration to write your own prayer of lament about a particular situation.

The Lament for Josseline was written about a young girl from Mexico who died in the desert in an attempt to get to the US. This lament was based on her story and a second story where individuals from Mexico were being trafficked into the US. The drivers of the 18-wheeler left it abandoned in the summer heat and nineteen died including a five-year-old boy found dead in his father's arms.

The Lament for Josseline

My heart mourns and my eyes are ever filled with tears images of
broken and lost children flash through my remembrance and
bring deep groans of sorrow to my lips.
Within my ears are the cries of the dying. I hear your daughter whisper,
"Mami, mami, mi estoy muriendo." (Mommy, mommy, I'm dying.)
And I am undone! We are a nation of greed.
We are a people of violence and hate.
We are a wicked people who leave fragile beautiful daughters to die in the deserts And
innocent baby sons to suffocate in tombs of deceit and greed.
Hear the cries of your daughters and sons. Hear the weeping of mothers and fathers.
Then redeem us oh Lord that we may be a nation that answers the cries of the oppressed.
Grant us courage to snatch back dying children from deserts and man-made tombs.
Bring healing to wounds that run too deep for words.
Oh Lord, rescue the rejected so the world will know your name.
Though we deserve your wrath, pour out mercy
And lead us into your promise of goodness and hope.
For you alone are God.
And you alone can redeem a land filled with the blood of babes.
Glory be to you God who hears the cries of the lost.

INTERCESSORY PRAYER

And we are confident that he hears us whenever we ask for anything that pleases him. And since we know he hears us when we make our requests, we also know that he will give us what we ask for.
1 John 5:14-15

Intercessory prayer may be one of the most familiar types of prayer. Praying for other people is important... especially for those we might tend to ignore unless prompted. As we pray for others our faith is increased as we draw close to God to know how to pray. It is also increased as we see how He uses and answers those prayers.

Three examples of how to pray intercessory prayers.

1. Simply pray how the individual has asked you to pray. That could be prayers for healing, or wisdom, or any variety of other issues.

2. Pray as the Holy Spirit leads. Spend time in the presence of God and ask Holy Spirit how to pray over an individual, leader, city, or nation.

3. Pray the word of God. This is a powerful method of praying for others. Find scriptures that address the purpose of prayer and insert the name of the individual, leader, city, or nation as you pray the scripture.

PRAYER OF THANKSGIVING

Give thanks to the Lord, for he is good! His faithful love endures forever.
Psalm 107:1

Come, let us sing to the Lord! Let us shout joyfully to the Rock of our salvation.
Let us come to him with thanksgiving. Let us sing psalms of praise to him.
For the Lord is a great God, a great King above all gods.
Psalm 95:1-3

Scripture teaches us to give thanks to God. There are many ways we can give thanks. Prayers of thanksgiving can be offered for the ways God has blessed us. We can be thankful for the amazing attributes of God demonstrated in our lives. We can pray in gratitude for the people in our lives. The main goal is to take time to reflect on areas to offer thanks.

Our prayer of thanksgiving can also take on different forms. We can write our prayers as a song, like the psalmist references above. We can create a list of all our blessings.

And at times, our prayer of thanksgiving can be for the struggles that teach us patience and draw us closer to God.

LECTIO DIVINA

For the word of God is alive and powerful. It is sharper than the sharpest two-edged sword, cutting between soul and spirit, between joint and marrow. It exposes our inner-most thoughts and desires.
Hebrews 4:12

Lectio Divina is Latin for "Divine Reading." This is a traditional monastic practice of scriptural reading, meditation, and prayer. The purpose is to promote communion with God and to increase the knowledge of God's word. We recognize that scripture is the divine word of God, but it is also considered the living word. And from beginning to end the Bible points to the fact that the written words of scripture are indelibly proclaiming Christ as the living word.

Steps for Lectio Divina

1. Reading. Read a passage slowly and carefully within the Bible.
2. Prayer. Having a loving conversation with God.
3. Meditation. Thinking deeply or dwelling upon a spiritual reality within a text.
4. Contemplation. Resting in God's presence.
5. Action. Go and do likewise.

Week 1
Sin

Sin

All harm, all conflict, all trauma is rooted in sin. Working with victims of violent crime, it is very easy to make the statement that the harm done to them or a loved one was due to the sin of the offender. There are times in families where it is easy to see the sin that lead to the conflict like adultery, or abuse rooted in anger and rage, or addiction.

Other times, the sin is less evident. In conflict between friends it may not be that one person set out to hurt the other, but even thoughtlessness can be rooted in sin. When we think of our needs over others, intentionally or not, it is selfish. It is vital in the peacemaking process for sin to be the starting place. It must be named; it must be called out in the fullness of what was done.

So often we want to rush toward reconciliation and restoration and we do not look at the ugliness. Because, face it, no one likes to look at their own messiness or wickedness. Yet, we all have failed and sinned. One of the frustrations of those oppressed by unjust systems is the lack acknowledgment of the sin of the oppressor. The same rings true in crime and family conflict. Have you ever said, or heard someone say, "Why can't they just admit what they did?" That question begs for the sin to be named.

This is so important in VOMD. If the offender does not take responsibility for the harm the process stops. In peacemaking, sin is the starting point. As you go through this week focus on the impact of sin in your relationships or in working with others experiencing injustice or oppression.

But the Lord said, "What have you done? Listen! Your brother's blood cries out to me from the ground! Now you are cursed and banished from the ground, which has swallowed your brother's blood."
Genesis 4:10-11

In this passage Jesus is called our mediator. Go back and read the story of Cain and Abel in Genesis 4:1-14.

This is the first story told about the firstborn of man. Remember Adam and Eve were simply created by God, not through birth in the union of man and woman like Cain and Abel. Do not miss the significance of the fact the first story about humanity is a story of the most violent crime of murder.

The journey of a peacemaker always finds the entrance at the place of sin. When sin came into the world, devastation and destruction followed. One cannot proceed with any journey toward peace without first naming, acknowledging, and lamenting the sins. These sins break unity, harmony, and usher in pain and sorrow.

Day 1

CENTERING PRAYER

First and foremost, our desire is to seek and sit in the presence of our loving Father. Begin this week with centering prayer. Remember to allow yourself to focus on being present with the Triune God: the Father, Jesus, and the Holy Spirit. If you are new to centering prayer start with five minutes. You can always increase the time as you learn to remain in his presence.

After your prayer time journal any thoughts you have about the day or week ahead.

Day 2

READ AND REFLECT

Power of Sin

His legs hung limply from the dining room table about a foot from the floor while his eyes locked on the pile of mac n' cheese and dinosaur nuggets on his plate. Typically, my seven-year-old son Trey would be shoving food into his mouth in huge gulps, but today he just sat and stared.

"Are you okay, Trey Bear?" I asked.

"I don't feel good," he replied. "My throat hurts."

I could tell he was not his usual self, so I asked if he would just like a glass of chocolate milk to help with his sore throat.

I expected his face to light up at the suggestion, but instead, he croaked out, "Can I please go lie down?"

Before I could answer, huge tears were streaming down his innocent face. I felt his forehead, and he had no fever, but I told him it was okay for him to go lie down.

A little while later, I went in to check on him. His bed was empty. Hearing sniffling and whimpers, I made a quick scan of the room. Small dirty toes peeked out of the shadows of the open closet. Looking in I saw Trey. His head was buried behind his knees where he sat tucked into the corner. I leaned in closer to see he was crying and asked him what was wrong.

"Mom, I have done something really bad," was his response.

"Tell me," I replied.

He went on to tell me a story about how he and his friend were playing and like typical kids found themselves in an argument. At one point, Trey swallowed hard as he tried to stop his tears and said, "Mom, I used the 'f' word."

"What do you mean? What 'f' word?"

Big brown eyes filled once again as he choked out the words, "You know… fart." It took everything I had not to laugh. But I had to keep a stern face because it was clear he felt horrible about using that word. And on top of that, he clearly thought "fart" was a cuss word.

Before I could reply he blurted out, "That's a sin, isn't it Mom?" I explained it was not a kind word, and if he knew it was wrong, he could simply pray and ask for forgiveness. He twisted his legs into a pretzel as he sat up and folded his chubby fingers in prayer. With squinted eyes and head bowed almost onto his lap, he prayed a sweet prayer asking God to forgive his sin.

I thought that was the end of the story. I also thought it was interesting that he was so bothered by the idea he had sinned. Little did I realize we were about to go on a three-week journey of confessions and repentance. I was started awake around 2:00 a.m. with Trey standing beside my bed weeping. Coming out of the haze, I was startled and grabbed him to console him.

After a few minutes, he blurted out, "Mom, I have sinned."

He went on to describe a time he was with his friend, and they were watching some workers doing renovations on a neighbor's house. At one point, when no one was watching, they decided to pour the can of Sprite they were drinking into a bucket of paint. In his retelling, he cried and said he knew it was wrong, and it was a terrible sin that he ruined that paint.

"I can't even tell the man I am sorry because he is gone. That's terrible, right Mom?"

I couldn't decide if I was irritated that he woke me in the middle of the night or if I was touched by the tenderness of his heart and the realization of his "sin." But like the day before, I reminded him he could pray and ask for forgiveness, which he did.

There were probably a dozen more episodes of the confessions of seven-year-old Trey. A few were serious like ruining the paint, but most only amounted to little-boy mischief. On one such confession, where he had climbed on a neighbor's roof, he could not be consoled with merely praying for forgiveness. He was convinced he needed to go to the neighbor and confess his sin. A slight knock on the door and Trey was facing Tom, our six-foot-five neighbor. He was a very kind man, but to Trey, he looked massive. Trey went on to confess his actions of being on the roof. Standing behind Trey, I shrugged and smiled in response to Tom's questioning eyes.

Tom knelt beside Trey and sternly said, " That could have been very dangerous and was wrong, but I forgive you. Just don't do it again."

Trey nodded and proclaimed loudly, "I won't!"

This season of confession and little-boy prayers of repentance went on for several weeks, and at times, Trey was physically nauseous. He confessed everything he could remember doing wrong for years. Finally, I sat him down and explained that confession was right and necessary, but if he didn't like the way it felt to sin, maybe he should think about his actions before he did something wrong. That piece of advice was accepted as if he had been given a gift of the most excellent value. He jumped up, hugged my neck, and with resolve, he ran off to play like a "good boy."

I often think of that time, and when I do, I am still in awe of my child's tender heart toward his sin. It led me to serious soul searching. Am I as sickened by my sin? Do I seek to repent and make things right when I have wronged others? Is my heart not satisfied until I speak words of repentance?

In our crazy divisive world, we could all learn a lesson from a little boy. We could all seek to have a heart that is sickened by our hurtful actions and words.

Reflections

What do you need to confess today?

How can words of repentance to the one you have wronged heal your heart?

Day 3

PRAYER OF LAMENT

How long, Lord? Will you forget me forever? How long will you hide your face from me? How long must I wrestle with my thoughts and day after day have sorrow in my heart? How long will my enemy triumph over me?
Look on me and answer, Lord my God. Give light to my eyes, or I will sleep in death, and my enemy will say, "I have overcome him," and my foes will rejoice when I fall. But I trust in your unfailing love; my heart rejoices in your salvation. I will sing the Lord's praise for he has been good to me.
Psalm 31

Reflect on a time you saw devastation caused by sin. It can be a time you realized the consequences of your own sin. It can be a time you saw, or knew, someone suffer devastation by the sin of another. It can be any situation where sin caused harm.

On the following page write your own Psalm of lament as your prayer for this sin. You can insert your name or the name of the individual into the words you write to make it more personal. Then, allow this Psalm to be your cry, your prayer of lament to your Father.

My Prayer of Lament

Day 4

INTERCESSORY PRAYER

Therefore, since we are surrounded by such a huge crowd of witnesses to the life of faith, let us strip off every weight that slows us down, especially the sin that so easily trips us up. And let us run with endurance the race God has set before us.
Hebrews 12:1

Conflicts and injustices are always linked to sin. We can see how the sin of one person causes harm and disharmony in relationships. Think of someone you know, whose "sin that trips them [us] up" is creating harm or division. Intercede for that person. Our natural instinct is to pray for those who have been harmed like we did yesterday. We also need to learn to intercede for those who create the harm. So pray for that person.

Begin with asking the Holy Spirit to show you how to pray for that person. Record what you receive.

If a scripture comes to mind about this person or the sin, use that as a way to pray. Record your intercessory prayer below.

Day 5

PRAYER OF THANKSGIVING

So now, since we have been made right in God's sight by faith in his promises, we can have real peace with him because of what Jesus Christ our Lord has done for us. For because of our faith, he has brought us into this place of highest privilege where we now stand, and we confidently and joyfully look forward to actually becoming all that God has had in mind for us to be.
Romans 5:1-2

While sin leaves a path of destruction that causes many to suffer, we have a Savior who leads us through the devastation to a place of peace and wholeness. Spend time today thanking him for all he has done for you and will do for others still tangled in sin's grip.

List several ways Christ has lead you through difficult times caused by sin:

Record your prayer of thanksgiving for the faithfulness Christ has, and continues, to show to you.

Day 6

LECTIO DIVINA

Read the following passages using the guide of Lectio Divina and record your thoughts. Read this passage slowly and carefully three times:

You have come to God, the Judge of all, to the spirits of the righteous made perfect, to Jesus the mediator of a new covenant, and to the sprinkled blood that speaks a better word than the blood of Abel.
Hebrews 12:21-24

What one word or phrase sticks out as you read God's word?

Ask why God prompted you with this word or phrase.

Then continue on the following page.

Meditation
Think deeply on the spiritual reality within the text. Record your thoughts.

Contemplation
Resting in God's presence. Be still and sit in God's presence for a few moments.

Action
Go and do likewise. What has this passage, prayer and quiet time with God inspired you to go and do? List any actions you are prompted to take.

Day 7

CONCLUDING PRAYER

Powerful God, your plans are not thwarted by the sins in our lives. You have given and loved us in ways we do not deserve. You see all that we are and all we are not. And yet you still call us to you.

Forgive our sins: for the things you asked us to do that we did not do, and the things you told us not to do but we did anyway.

Wonderful Father, you gave us heart to love and be loved. You command us to love you and to love others. Yet we fall short. We forget to seek the one who loves us above all others. And we hurt others by withholding the very love you gave to us.

Forgive our sins: for the things you asked us to do that we did not do, and the things you told us not to do but we did anyway.

Everlasting Savior, we come to you and confess our sin. Our journey begins with sin but may it end in mercy. Pour out your mercy on us. And may we pour out the same mercy on others.

Forgive our sins: for the things you asked us to do that we did not do, and the things you told us not to do but we did anyway.

Beautiful Creator, we join you on this journey of peace. Allow us to grow past, and in spite of, our shortcomings. Teach us to freely give as we have been given so others experience the ever-present love and faithfulness to those you call your own.

Blessed be our Christ who gave his life that we may receive the gift of forgiveness.

Week 2
Truth

Truth

Once sin is acknowledged we move toward truth. When working with victims of violent crime, it is common to hear statements like, "I just want them to know what they've taken from me." It's one thing for offenders to admit they committed the crime that devastated another, it is a completely different thing for them to embrace the full impact of that harm. Truth must be spoken for healing to begin. This is a challenge for many because if feels like placing labels on people. It is easy to understand that the mother of a murdered child would place the label "murderer" on the one who killed her child. Or the survivor of sexual assault places the label "rapist" on the one who committed the assault. Most of the time, the hesitancy to look fully at the sin is linked to shame. But the truth can be discussed and the fullness of the ugliness of sin be brought to light, in spite of the shame.

It feels like judgment to use words like murderer or rapist. But the reality is that is the truth. In fact, it is not judgment; it is quite the opposite. Imagine the relief that can be found allowing someone to fully confess the harm they have done and be met with eyes of compassion and forgiveness. When that happens, shame loses its grip.

These first two topics point to some powerful questions that need to be asked. Are sin and truth, or lack thereof, the root of ongoing riots in our nation? Are those rioting angry and frustrated because those oppressing and harming will not acknowledge their sin? Are they angry that their voices in the fullness of the truth of the harm and trauma are not being heard?

Christ is a beautiful example of this. His resurrection was a beautiful and glorious miracle. But remember, the resurrection followed the crucifixion. The fullness and ugliness of sin was place on him on that cross. He willingly took on the sin, the shame, and the labels that didn't even belong to him. Three days later he rose and sin, death, and shame lost their grip.

But this is what you must do: Tell the truth to each other. Render verdicts in your courts that are just and that lead to peace.
Zechariah 8:16

Truth is a place of encounter for those seeking peace. So often, conflicts arise from the falsification or distortion of truth. There are a multitude of reasons people lie: fear, embarrassment, jealousy, power. The list goes on and on. When working as a peacemaker, truth becomes the gold mined. This phase of facilitation can take time and often feels like digging up boulders. Truth should not be sought for the purpose of proving who is right and who is wrong. Truth should be sought to become the foundation for repairing damaged relationships. Any other foundation will fail.

This week the prayers will focus on truth from several perspectives. There are times when truth is distorted for the purpose of power and oppression. There are times when truth is denied out of fear. There are times truth is hidden with no bad intentions. In all these circumstances the fact remains, truth is not evident and because of that, harm is done. As you go through this week, seek to mine the depths for truth of those in your life and those who will ask for your help as a peacemaker.

Day 1

CENTERING PRAYER

First and foremost, our desire is to seek and sit in the presence of our loving Father. Begin this week with centering prayer. Remember to allow yourself to focus on being present with the Triune God: the Father, Jesus, and the Holy Spirit. If you are new to centering prayer start with five minutes. You can always increase the time as you learn to remain in his presence.

After your prayer time journal any thoughts you have about the day or week ahead.

Day 2

READ AND REFLECT

The Devastation of Lies

Kim's breathing was shallow and she shuffled her feet as she slowly made her way down the long sidewalk to the interior of a maximum-security prison. She was here to meet with the man convicted of raping her fifteen years earlier. She had been working with a mediator for six months to prepare for this face-to-face victim offender mediation.

She knew this day was going to be emotional and frightening, but she didn't realize it would be this difficult. Her mediator explained they didn't have to go on, that she could stop if it was too much. As much as Kim wanted to run back to her car and drive home, she knew she needed to continue. She needed to sit in front of Arthur, the man who raped her and tell him how his actions impacted her life and future.

Kim and Arthur were close friends prior to the rape. It was after a night of hanging out with friends that her world was devastated. They were drinking and everyone crashed in different corners of her parents' house since they were away on a cruise for two more days. She was startled awake by something heavy on her chest. As the fog in her mind cleared she laughed realizing it was Arthur trying to be stupid. But within seconds, he covered her face and was pulling her skirt up. She kept waiting for him to jump up and start laughing but he didn't. She tried to get him off her but his two-hundred-and-fifty-pound athletic body was no match for her. She wept as he continued to violate her.

The next few months went from horrible to nightmarish. She reported the rape and Arthur was arrested. As expected, he denied any rape and said their encounter was consensual. The evidence of massive bruises was proof it wasn't. The rape was devastating but what made her life unbearable in the years afterward was the betrayal of her friends. Arthur lied and told everybody she made the whole thing up. His charisma made it easy for all her friends to believe him over her. Some days it was more difficult to deal with the looks and hateful comments of her now former friends than it was to deal with the actual assault.

Now years later, her hope was that he would finally tell the truth. After signing all the paperwork required for the mediation Kim sat at the square picnic table in the prison visitation room. Her trembling fingers were tucked under her legs. She was determined not to show Arthur how frightened she was. Finally, he was escorted into the room and the mediation began.

He sat and listened to all Kim had to say. He heard how their former friends made her life so miserable she eventually had to move to another city. After listening to all he had done, he said he was so deeply sorry for what he did to her that night. He wept as he told her how he knew she hadn't lied, he knew exactly what he had done. He also knew that his lies would hurt but never realized until this day, just how much he had taken from her.

Through tears he asked, "Is there anything I can do that would make things better?"

Instantly she replied, "Yes. Tell the truth."

He nodded his head and said he would, that it was the least he could do. He told her he would write to his family and tell them he had lied all those years ago. He would admit to them he had raped Kim and lied all this time. He also agreed to write to the few friends who remained in contact with him.

Now it was Kim's turn to cry. Never in a million years did she think he would tell the truth. And now, hearing the words, she knew things would be different. There was no going back and repairing relationships from the past, but the idea that the truth would be told was a gift Kim never thought she'd receive.

The mediation lasted a few minutes longer and they wrapped up the time together. After more paperwork and debriefing questions, it was time to leave. Kim and her mediator made their way back out of the prison. This time Kim skipped like a child as she walked down that same long sidewalk leading to her new life.

Answer reflection questions on the following page.

Reflections

Are there areas in your life where you sought truth and have not found it? How does that impact you?

Are there individuals in your sphere of influence that have been oppressed by lies? If so, how can you pray for them? How can you bring truth into those spaces?

Day 3

PRAYER OF LAMENT

The LORD detests lying lips, but he delights in those who tell the truth.
Proverbs 12:22

But those plotting to destroy me will come to ruin. They will go down into the depths of the earth. They will die by the sword and become the food of jackals. But the king will rejoice in God. All who swear to tell the truth will praise him, while liars will be silenced.
Psalm 63:9-11

There are several ways to approach this lament. Choose one or more of the following options:
1. Think of a time you were deeply hurt by lies that has not been set right. Write a lament about the pain and a cry for truth.
2. Think of a people group that has been oppressed by lies of those in power. Write a lament for their suffering and a cry for truth.
3. Think of a time you lied to someone. Write a lament for the one you hurt with a cry for healing.

On the following page write your own Psalm of lament as your prayer for pain caused by untruth. You can insert your name or the name of the individual into the words you write to make it more personal. Then, allow this Psalm to be your cry, your prayer of lament to your Father.

My Prayer of Lament

Day 4

INTERCESSORY PRAYER

Jesus said to the people who believed in him, "You are truly my disciples if you remain faithful to my teachings. And you will know the truth, and the truth will set you free."
John 8:31-32

There are multiple individuals and groups of people who have been victims of lies. These can be historical lies that are widely believed but are not grounded in truth. Those forms of falsehood are designed to oppress. Pray for those who have been oppressed by lies.

Even more challenging is to pray for those believing and spreading lies. Pray that they will know the truth and that truth will set them free to then bring freedom to the oppressed.

Begin with asking the Holy Spirit to show you how to pray. Record what you receive.

If a scripture comes to mind about those impacted by lies, use that as a way to pray. Record your intercessory prayer below.

Day 5

PRAYER OF THANKSGIVING

When the Spirit of truth comes, he will guide you into all truth. He will not speak on his own but will tell you what he has heard. He will tell you about the future.
John 16:13

Make a list of the times and ways the Holy Spirit has been your guide and lead you to truth. These can be moments when you lied, knew it was wrong, and set things right. It can be times when the Holy Spirit opened your eyes to see lies you believed. It can be times the Spirit revealed truth to you through his word.

List several ways Christ has lead you through difficult times caused by lies:

Write your prayer of thanksgiving for the ways the Holy Spirit has lead you to truth.

Day 6

LECTIO DIVINA

Read the following passages using the guide of Lectio Divina and record your thoughts. Read this passage slowly and carefully three times:

Then we will no longer be immature like children. We won't be tossed and blown about by every wind of new teaching. We will not be influenced when people try to trick us with lies so clever they sound like the truth. Instead, we will speak the truth in love, growing in every way more and more like Christ, who is the head of his body, the church. He makes the whole body fit together perfectly. As each part does its own special work, it helps the other parts grow, so that the whole body is healthy and growing and full of love.
Ephesians 4:14-16

What one word or phrase sticks out as you read God's word?

Ask why God prompted you with this word or phrase.

Then continue on the following page.

Meditation
Think deeply on the spiritual reality within the text. Record your thoughts.

Contemplation
Resting in God's presence. Be still and sit in God's presence for a few moments.

Action
Go and do likewise. What has this passage, prayer and quiet time with God inspired you to go and do? List any actions you are prompted to take.

Day 7
CONCLUDING PRAYER

Lord, write your own words upon our hearts and inscribe them on our lips. Give us a hunger for truth. Stir our hearts with a desire to bring truth where lies have prevailed.

O God of Truth, guide us, lead us, illuminate our paths. Show us your truth.

Show us times our words have been deceptive, hurtful, injuring others, lacking mercy and grace. Give us courage to confess and strive to make right the wrongs we have done.

O God of Truth, guide us, lead us, illuminate our paths. Show us your truth.

Help us to charge the gates for those held in bondage by lies. Give us power and strength as we seek to release the captives. Help us to love and embrace them, fully restored.

O God of Truth, guide us, lead us, illuminate our paths. Show us your truth.

Guide us to speak truth in love to those spreading lies, that they may repent. Then give us hearts to love those who had once been the oppressors.

O God of Truth, guide us, lead us, illuminate our paths. Show us your truth.

Lord God, let the words of our mouths and the meditations of our hearts be acceptable in your sight, O Lord, our Rock and Redeemer.

O God of Truth, guide us, lead us, illuminate our paths. Show us your truth.

Week 3
Repentence

Repentance

Once truth is spoken the one who harmed the other has a choice, an opportunity to repent. The important element in repentance is the turning away from sin. The sinner, fully understanding the implications of the sin and harm done, acknowledges that harm, acknowledges the responsibility for the harm. But repentance also requires a commitment to turn away from the sin and not repeat the harmful action in the future.

Repentance occurs in the present but includes both the past and the future. Admitting to harm in the past, committing to change, and turning away from the sin in the future are essential. If there is no repentance, the future holds the possibility of continued harm. In cases of violent crime or serious harm, repentance is vital.

Sadly, there are times when truth is spoken but the guilty person refuses to acknowledge the harm. Unless the person who sinned acknowledges what he or she did, how do you know it will not happen again? It would be foolish to continue to risk ongoing abuse and harm. It becomes very challenging to reconcile and have a healthy relationship with someone who had wronged you in the past. With repentance, there is assurance that the offender is on notice not to repeat the offense. Repentance moves us forward toward healing and reconciliation, and is required to move beyond the damage with full willingness, committing to turn away from future harm.

Now I am glad I sent it, not because it hurt you, but because the pain caused you to repent and change your ways. It was the kind of sorrow God wants his people to have, so you were not harmed by us in any way. For the kind of sorrow God wants us to experience leads us away from sin and results in salvation. There's no regret for that kind of sorrow. But worldly sorrow, which lacks repentance, results in spiritual death. Just see what this godly sorrow produced in you! Such earnestness, such concern to clear yourselves, such indignation, such alarm, such longing to see me, such zeal, and such a readiness to punish wrong. You showed that you have done everything necessary to make things right.
2 Corinthians 7:9-11

There is a distinct difference between remorse and repentance. This passage defines that difference. Remorse is the first step toward repentance. It usually begins with getting caught or suffering consequences for wrong action. Statements like "I am so sorry I hurt you" are words of remorse. But being remorseful does not require the turning away from sin. Repentance does. Paul illustrated that worldly sorrow or remorse that lacks repentance "leads to death," hidden with no bad intentions. In all these circumstances the fact remains, truth is not evident and because of that, harm is done. As you go through this week, seek to mine the depths for truth of those in your life and those who will ask for your help as a peacemaker.

Day 1

CENTERING PRAYER

First and foremost, our desire is to seek and sit in the presence of our loving Father. Begin this week with centering prayer. Remember to allow yourself to focus on being present with the Triune God: the Father, Jesus, and the Holy Spirit. If you are new to centering prayer start with five minutes. You can always increase the time as you learn to remain in his presence.

After your prayer time journal any thoughts you have about the day or week ahead.

Day 2

READ AND REFLECT

Reflection of Truth

Creepy, was the first thought Clara had as the three men walked into the room to sit at the large plastic white table. All three were part of an offender panel about to speak at the Victim Offender Mediation Symposium.

Clara spoke earlier on a victim impact panel about surviving childhood sexual abuse of her father. She wanted to rush back to her hotel room and sit alone in the dark to calm down. But instead, this afternoon, a friend insisted she sit in on the offender panel workshop. The room for the session was tiny. Clara sat on the back row with her back against the wall. She scanned the space and noticed the room was beginning to fill. If she wanted to leave and skip this session, it would have to be soon. Just as she was about to head out, her friend walked in and sat next to her. She was stuck and had to stay.

The first person to speak was a tall, lanky man named Jonathan. His salt and pepper hair had already receded several inches. It didn't help that he wore black-rim glasses that reminded her of Mr. Reed Minor, her nerdy algebra teacher from ninth grade. His wrinkled plaid shirt had seen a few too many washings.

Something about him was unsettling for Clara. The moderator asked Jonathan to talk about his crime.

"I sexually assaulted my six-year-old daughter," he hesitated before adding, "for over four years."

Clara stopped breathing. Her eyes transfixed on Jonathan. The soft touch from her friend on her arm made Clara gasp and realize she had not been breathing. Jonathan continued to describe the crime he committed. His wife had an affair and left him for another man. She left everything behind, including their two small daughters. It was about a year after the divorce that Jonathan began to watch his daughter, Lily. He explained that he knew the way he looked at her was wrong. And that was when the lies in his head began. She looked at him the same way he looked at her. She really wanted him to be closer. She needed him to love her more.

After several months of trying to resist the lies, he gave in. He explained how he finally went into her small bedroom that first night over ten years ago. Those words plummeted Clara into a panic. She frantically looked around the room, worried the screams in her ears had been heard by others in the room. No one was moving, so she realized the sound was in her head. Jonathan went on to say how he knew when he walked through his daughter's door what he was about to do was evil and horribly wrong. He cried as he explained that he knew he was sick and how much he had destroyed his daughter's life. He wept as he recounted her haunted eyes those nights in her room, knowing he was the monster in her life.

That was it, Clara was undone. Her eyes darted from Jonathan to the door. Why did they put the table between the audience and the door? There was no escape. She was trapped. The pounding and throbbing of her pulse in her ears, she glanced at her friend and saw the concern in her eyes. She knew. She knew and was unable to help Clara escape. Alarms were sounding in her mind as she tried not to drown in her hysteria.

> Her eyes went back to Jonathan, and she heard him say the words, "I am so ashamed of what I did."

Two possible actions flashed in Clara's mind at the hearing of those words. One was of rushing up to the table, digging her fingers into Jonathan's face and gouging out his eyes. The other was to rush to the table and kiss Jonathan's cheek. The reality that she wanted both of those things simultaneously was almost unbearable. But it was the truth. She hated him for what he represented, for what he did. But she also loved him for admitting the wrong he had done. In that realization, she surrendered. She closed her eyes and willed herself to breathe until this nightmare was over. Fifteen minutes later, she was surrounded by only her close friends and counselor. She didn't know what next steps she should take but she knew this encounter would change her life forever.

Answer reflection questions on the following page.

Reflections

What is the distinction that made Jonathan repentant and not just remorseful?

Are there places in your life where you need to move from remorse to repentance?

Day 3

PRAYER OF LAMENT

You do not desire a sacrifice, or I would offer one. You do not want a burnt offering. The sacrifice you desire is a broken spirit. You will not reject a broken and repentant heart, O God. Look with favor on Zion and help her; rebuild the walls of Jerusalem. Then you will be pleased with sacrifices offered in the right spirit— with burnt offerings and whole burnt offerings. Then bulls will again be sacrificed on your altar.
Psalm 51:16-19

Is there a situation in your life where you need to repent? Ask the Holy Spirit to lead you into truth about places you need to repent. Write all that comes to mind.

Repent, then write a prayer of lament over that area of your life.

Day 4

INTERCESSORY PRAYER

Whoever conceals their sins does not prosper, but the one who confesses and renounces them finds mercy.
Proverbs 28:13

Addiction is also a place where the distinction between remorse and repentance can be seen. Many addicts are keenly aware their actions hurt those they love and will be truly remorseful and say, "I am so sorry I hurt you like that."

But when they continue in that addiction, their behavior demonstrates a lack of repentance and not turning away from the addiction. Do you know someone trapped in the remorse of addiction and needing repentance? Intercede for that individual.

Or, has someone hurt you and been remorseful but not repentant? An example could be someone who said something hurtful and was remorseful, but then continued to say hurtful things. Pray for that individual.

Begin with asking the Holy Spirit to show you how to pray for this person. Record what you receive.

If a scripture comes to mind about this person, use that as a way to pray. Record your intercessory prayer below.

Day 5

PRAYER OF THANKSGIVING

*For I take no pleasure in the death of anyone, declares the Sovereign Lord.
Repent and live!*
Ezekiel 18:32

*"The time has come," he said. "The kingdom of God has come near. Repent and
believe the good news!"*
Mark 1:15

Think of times you moved beyond remorse into repentance. How did your turning away from sin bring new life? Write a prayer of thanksgiving for ALL the times you received new life after repentance.

Record your prayer of thanksgiving for the faithfulness Christ has, and continues, to show to you.

Day 6

LECTIO DIVINA

Read the following passages using the guide of Lectio Divina and record your thoughts. Read this passage slowly and carefully three times:

Don't tear your clothing in your grief, but tear your hearts instead. Return to the Lord your God, for he is merciful and compassionate, slow to get angry and filled with unfailing love. He is eager to relent and not punish.
Joel 2:13

What one word or phrase sticks out as you read God's word?

Ask why God prompted you with this word or phrase.

Then continue on the following page.

Meditation

Think deeply on the spiritual reality within the text. Record your thoughts.

Contemplation

Resting in God's presence. Be still and sit in God's presence for a few moments.

Action

Go and do likewise. What has this passage, prayer and quiet time with God inspired you to go and do? List any actions you are prompted to take.

Day 7

CONCLUDING PRAYER

Gracious God, we bow before you today. Your Son, our Savior Jesus, began his ministry by calling people to repentance: "Repent, for the kingdom of heaven is at hand."

God of mercy, we confess our sinfulness, our hurtful words and actions. Forgive us and help us turn from this sin.

Jesus promised that he came for us in our brokenness and sin. "I have not come to call the righteous but sinners to repentance."

God of mercy, we confess our sinfulness, our hurtful words and actions. Forgive us and help us turn from this sin.

Our Savior made it clear that God delights in us when we return to him. Yet, we have often failed to share the Good News of your love with others even though you made your will very clear.

God of mercy, we confess our sinfulness, our hurtful words and actions. Forgive us and help us turn from this sin.

So, forgive us and renew us, O Lord. Draw us to you through Jesus Christ our Savior. Rekindle our trust in you and our love for one another.

God of mercy, we confess our sinfulness, our hurtful words and actions. Forgive us and help us turn from this sin.

By your grace and Spirit, let us live as ones who have been crucified with Christ—so that it is no longer we who live, but Christ who lives in us. Wake us up.

God of mercy, we confess our sinfulness, our hurtful words and actions. Forgive us and help us turn from this sin.

Week 4
Forgiveness

Forgiveness

Forgiveness can be tricky business. Most people are eager and yearn for forgiveness when we have harmed another. But offering forgiveness to those who harmed is another thing all together. Yet freedom is found in that offering.

Forgiveness and repentance are delicately linked. When repentance is withheld, forgiveness is much more challenging if not impossible, particularly when the harm is substantial. Yet even when there is remorse and a commitment to change it can still be challenging to forgive.

In the center of the word "forgiveness" is the word "give." It is incredibly challenging to give something to someone who has harmed you. The truth is we would prefer to "get" something from that person. Get back what was taken. Get an honest answer. Get a commitment to never harm again. Get compensation for the damage done.

A unique trait of forgiveness is that it cannot be demanded. In actuality it must be discovered. Oh, yes, it is very clear that the Bible tells us to forgive others. But how the person who is harmed arrives at that conclusion is a very personal internal journey. So many times, over the years, victims have made statements like, "I know I need to forgive him, but I just don't know how." or "I am just not ready yet."

As peacemakers, we must be willing to allow those harmed by others the grace to discover forgiveness gently. Avoid phrases like, "You need to forgive and move on." Most victims have heard that exact statement and replied with, "Tell me how and I will." Listening is one of the best gifts we can give to one who is hurting. Sometimes it is in the retelling that the hurt finds forgiveness.

Then Peter came to Jesus and asked, "Lord, how many times shall I forgive my brother or sister who sins against me? Up to seven times?" Jesus answered, "I tell you, not seven times, but seventy-seven times.
Matthew. 18:21-22

Forgiveness is an act that can be the most desired and most dreaded. When we have hurt someone else we long for them to forgive us. When we are hurt, especially when we are deeply wounded, we may dread the idea of forgiving the one who hurt us.

The hate and rhetoric of polarizing issues on social media is rampant. Everyone has an opinion and wants to make that opinion know at any expense, even if it means hurting someone. All you have to do is turn on the news and injustice becomes evident. We are called to address injustice. Micah 6:8 tells us "to do what is right, to love mercy, and to walk humbly with your God." Sometimes loving mercy and walking humbly includes forgiving the one who hurts and has wronged us. We can still seek justice and do what is right, but we can also forgive.

The Read and Reflect for this week offers a powerful story of how forgiveness is offered in the darkest situations.

Day 1

CENTERING PRAYER

First and foremost, our desire is to seek and sit in the presence of our loving Father. Begin this week with centering prayer. Remember to allow yourself to focus on being present with the Triune God: the Father, Jesus, and the Holy Spirit. If you are new to centering prayer start with five minutes. You can always increase the time as you learn to remain in his presence.

After your prayer time journal any thoughts you have about the day or week ahead.

Day 2

READ AND REFLECT

Abide in Love

"I think you need to ask me for forgiveness." Alicia made this statement to Michael, the man that murdered her son. He sat on the other side of the glass in a tiny metal booth speaking to Alicia via the phone on the wall. They could not sit face to face since Michael was in prison not only for the murder but in administrative segregation, or ad seg. Ad seg is the section of the prison reserved for the most dangerous offenders.

Michael did not respond to her request. Instead, he dropped his eyes and asked a question in an attempt to change the conversation. Alicia answered his question, appearing to let it go.

As the mediator assigned to the case, I thought it was so strange that Alicia was even asking him that question. She had said many times in the previous months as we prepared for the meeting that she had forgiven Michael. During the victim impact statement she read at his sentencing, she forgave Michael. And even this morning she reminded him that she had forgiven him. But oddly here in the cramped, awkward space, she was requesting he ask her for forgiveness.

After a few minutes, she said again, "I think you need to ask me for forgiveness."

Alicia sat on the metal stool welded to the ground inside the booth. I sat crammed behind her with the metal door that locked us both in the booth on my other side. I could not see Alicia's face. But I could see Michael.

When she repeated her statement a second time, he dropped his eyes again and breathed out the words, "I don't feel I have the right."

He changed the subject again and began talking about details of the crime. Alicia followed the conversation. She asked questions and he gave answers.

Finally, a third time, Alicia said, "I think you need to ask me for forgiveness." Realizing she was not going to let this go, Michael lowered his head. I wondered if he was searching his soul to see if those words were a part of his reality. It was probably only a few seconds but in his searching, time slowed to a drag.

He took a deep breath and laboriously pushed out the words, "Will you forgive me?"

Immediately she answered, "Yes."

I watched the strong, muscular, and hard-faced young man melt. Tears burst from his eyes. Huge tears flooded his cheeks and fell into pools under his chin. His body heaved spastically with deep sobbing. Eventually, he regained some semblance of composure.

Michael and Alicia spoke gently for the remaining minutes. They both stood to leave, and as a parting gesture, Alicia placed her hand on the cold glass. Michael raised his hand and set it opposite of hers. Then we left. The meeting ended.

Afterward, I asked Alicia about the purpose of her request for Michael to ask for forgiveness. Notably, in light of the fact she had already forgiven him.

She quickly responded. "I didn't do that for me. I did that for him." I followed up by asking what she felt when she made that request.

Timidly, she answered, "Love? Does that make me crazy?"

I replied to her question, "I think what I just witnessed was the most beautiful demonstration of what it means to love our enemies." Here was a woman who had experienced the most horrific ordeal in the murder of her child. She had every right to hate Michael. But, she acted in love.

Alicia and Michael remind us of an encounter that occurred hundreds of years ago, a meeting that took place between the resurrected Christ and his disciple Peter. Peter displayed cowardice and betrayal to his Master, to Christ—betrayed him not once, but three times. Peter encountered the living Christ after the resurrection. When he did, three times Jesus asked him a question, "Peter, do you love me?"

Reflecting back over the times in my life where I experienced hurt and betrayal, I wonder, can I follow the example Alicia demonstrated that day in a prison visitation booth? I know I have no choice.

"I forgive you" are hard words to speak. Even harder is to demonstrate love to the ones who hurt us. Some days, "I love you" are the most troublesome words to say. Nevertheless, they can be the most cleansing to our soul.

Answer reflection questions on the following page.

Reflections

Who do you need to seek to confess and ask for forgiveness?

And whom must you forgive? Journal your thoughts on what that means.

Day 3

PRAYER OF LAMENT

Have mercy on me, O God, according to your unfailing love; according to your great compassion blot out my transgressions. Wash away all my iniquity and cleanse me from my sin. For I know my transgressions, and my sin is always before me. Against you, you only, have I sinned and done what is evil in your sight; so you are right in your verdict and justified when you judge. Surely I was sinful at birth, sinful from the time my mother conceived me. Yet you desired faithfulness even in the womb; you taught me wisdom in that secret place.
Psalm 51

Reflect on a time you caused pain to someone you loved. Be honest and open with yourself before your merciful Father.

On the following page write your own Psalm of lament using Psalm 51 as your guide. Write a prayer of lament to the one you hurt as your prayer for this sin. You can insert your name or the name of the individual into the words you write to make it more personal. Then, allow this Psalm to be your cry, your prayer of lament to your Father.

My Prayer of Lament

Day 4

INTERCESSORY PRAYER

And when you stand praying, if you hold anything against anyone, forgive them, so that your Father in heaven may forgive you your sins.
Mark 11:25

You have heard that it was said, "Love your neighbor and hate your enemy." But I tell you, love your enemies and pray for those who persecute you, that you may be children of your Father in heaven. He causes his sun to rise on the evil and the good, and sends rain on the righteous and the unrighteous.
Matthew 5:43-45

One of the most challenging commands given to us in God's word is to love our enemies. Whether it is a wrong that causes us to hold a grudge or a devastating crime of betrayal that caused deep pain, our responsibility remains to forgive.

Think of a time you were hurt by another. If you haven't forgiven and find it a challenge to forgive that person, a good first step it to begin to simply pray. Begin with asking the Holy Spirit to show you how to pray for that person. Record what you receive.

If a scripture comes to mind about this person or the harm done, use that as a way to pray. Record your intercessory prayer below.

Day 5

PRAYER OF THANKSGIVING

As far as the east is from the west, so far has he removed our transgressions from us.
Psalm 103:12

Reflect back on times you were offered forgiveness by someone you hurt. What did their forgiveness mean to you? Make a list of all the times you can remember being forgiven by others.

Also, reflect back on all the times you have asked God for forgiveness. Then spend time thanking him for the richness of forgiveness.

Record your prayer of thanksgiving for the faithfulness Christ has, and continues, to show to you.

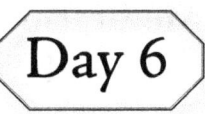

LECTIO DIVINA

Read the following passages using the guide of Lectio Divina and record your thoughts. Read this passage slowly and carefully three times:

For he has rescued us from the dominion of darkness and brought us into the kingdom of the Son he loves, in whom we have redemption, the forgiveness of sins.
Colossians 1:13-14

What one word or phrase sticks out as you read God's word?

Ask why God prompted you with this word or phrase.

Then continue on the following page.

Meditation

Think deeply on the spiritual reality within the text. Record your thoughts.

Contemplation

Resting in God's presence. Be still and sit in God's presence for a few moments.

Action

Go and do likewise. What has this passage, prayer and quiet time with God inspired you to go and do? List any actions you are prompted to take.

Day 7

CONCLUDING PRAYER

Powerful God, your plans are not thwarted by our sin. You have loved us in ways we do not deserve. You see all that we are and all we are not. And yet you still call us to you.

Forgive our sins: for the things you asked us to do that we did not do, and the things you told us not to do but we did anyway.

Wonderful Father, you gave us hearts to love and be loved. You command us to love you and to love others. Yet we fall short. We forget to seek the one who loves us above all others. And we hurt others by withholding the very love you gave to us.

Forgive our sins: for the things you asked us to do that we did not do, and the things you told us not to do but we did anyway.

Everlasting Savior, we come to you and confess our sin. Our journey begins with sin but may it end in mercy. Pour out your mercy on us. And may we pour out the same mercy on others.

Forgive our sins: for the things you asked us to do that we did not do, and the things you told us not to do but we did anyway.

Beautiful Creator, we join you on this journey of peace. Allow us to grow past, and in spite of, our shortcomings. Teach us to freely give as we have been given so others experience your ever-present love and faithfulness to those you call your own.

Blessed be our Christ who gave his life that we may receive the amazing gift of forgiveness.

Week 5
Reconciliation

Reconciliation

The story of the Good Samaritan teaches us about reconciliation. A typical focus is how the needs of the wounded man were met by the Good Samaritan while the other two chose not to help and even crossed to the opposite side of the road. However, it is important to remember that this story begins with a crime. Crime has a way of bringing about fear in people. We don't want to look too closely at crime because of the dangers involved. Fear can prevent us from looking into the face of crime because we realize it could just as easily happen to our loved ones or to us.

The Good Samaritan saw the victim's wounds were physical and extensive, so he took the man to an inn to be cared for. That act of taking the wounded man to a place to be cared for and restored or "brought back to a former state of harmony" is a form of reconciliation.

There are so many people in our churches, in our neighborhoods, and in our workplaces who are like the man on the side of the road but with wounds that are not visible. We can see evidence of their "woundedness" in the form of addiction, broken relationships, abuse, and depression. We are called to help bring people back to that "former state of harmony." We can bring healing those who are suffering injustices and oppression right here on the highways and byways of our own communities.

Therefore, if you are offering your gift at the altar and there remember that your brother or sister has something against you, leave your gift there in front of the altar. First go and be reconciled to them; then come and offer your gift.
Matthew 5:23-24

The term "reconciliation" has multiple meanings that are used in a variety of contexts. In some contexts, the term evokes a positive response, such as when it is used in reference to humankind being made right with God. In other contexts, the term evokes a negative response. For example, if reconciliation is used in reference to attempts to bring closure to deeply traumatic events such as the Trail of Tears or chattel slavery in the United States, it could delegitimize the significance of the harm and minimize the ongoing struggle of those impacted.

The scripture above references a conflict between individuals that must be addressed before bringing an offering to God. It requires the physical action of going and speaking with a brother or sister to address an offense. When we seek to reconcile with each other, it allows us to enter more freely and rightly into worship with God.

Day 1

CENTERING PRAYER

First and foremost, our desire is to seek and sit in the presence of our loving Father. Begin this week with centering prayer. Remember to allow yourself to focus on being present with the Triune God: the Father, Jesus, and the Holy Spirit. If you are new to centering prayer start with five minutes. You can always increase the time as you learn to remain in his presence.

After your prayer time journal any thoughts you have about the day or week ahead.

Day 2

READ AND REFLECT

Hidden Treasure and a Buckskin Dun

There is a man named Thomas who is my friend. We met in a prison in Texas while preparing for a face-to-face meeting with the son of the man he murdered. It was not the details in the mediation that stood out in this particular meeting with the old man. He told me many stories of his life, but the following story struck a chord in my heart. It was profound to hear the wisdom from this former death-row inmate and see how his insight beautifully highlights the need and power of reconciliation.

Thomas was a boy who lived in a small dusty town in South Texas. He was a typical boy with dreams in his heart and energy in his boots. His greatest dream was to buy a horse and learn to rope calves. He worked several summers at odd jobs like mowing lawns and sacking groceries at the local supermarket until he had enough money to start living his dream.

With a puffed-out chest, cash in his pocket and a grin stretching across his face the boy headed to the monthly horse auction. He tried to walk steady, looking mature, but there was just no containing the occasional skip that interrupted his stride. He was going to buy his horse. He saw the exquisite horse, though clearly green, what he called a buckskin dun.

That sunny morning, seeing that raw animal kicking against its handler, he knew he had to have her. Being fresh and young there was never a doubt he could train this scrappy mare. And at the end of the day, with $300 less in his pocket, the boy headed home with his buckskin dun. Well, actually, he learned later she was a just a dun, but he always liked calling her his "buckskin dun."

    He worked with his horse every day. He was gentle but demanding. After weeks of work, the boy was ready to saddle the dun and try to rope the mangled wooden calf he had built from scrap two-by-fours and an old cow skull. He stood next to the buckskin dun and whispered into her flicking ear. He could see in her eyes that she wanted to please him. And indeed, she did.

    But as time went on, the boy began to wander from his dreams and his dun. Drinking and trouble came all too easy and lead him into dangerous choices. Everything stopped on the day he killed a man. His days in that small town ended when he left to serve out his life in prison. Eventually, his family sold the dun back to the horse trader. But the horse was different. No matter how hard the man tried, the buckskin dun never worked for him like she had for the boy. Eventually, the horse was turned out to pasture where she died under a twisted tree in the back corner. Farmhands on that ranch said you could see a loneliness in the eyes of the dun.

    The boy, now man, was like his horse eating his crow of loneliness daily. He longed for the times before his dark choices. He would have died the same lonely death of his horse had it not been for a glimmer of hope he found one night in a cement room at the end of a cold corridor on death row. The night he met his Savior and knew he had found life.

The old man finished his story and looked at me.

With glistening eyes he whispered, "They say there are more buried treasures in cemeteries than anywhere else."

His heart ached knowing that the buckskin dun's talent and ability turned to dust under that tree. And he knew his time would come as well. But he was committed to live with the purpose of giving away the many treasures life had given him, even in the harsh world of a Texas prison.

And he did just that with the son of the man he murdered. He gave him the only treasures he had to give: his regret, his sorrow, his remorse. The son had not expected the thin-skinned man with missing teeth and gentle words. He had expected the monster from his nightmares as a boy without his father. Instead the son and the man sat two feet apart sharing deep sorrow. In the wrinkled face of humanity, the son found the gift of forgiveness.

I left that meeting in wonder. The metal gate with razor wire shut noisily behind me as I left my friend in his cement home. That clanging stirred me to think, who needs me to drop everything to go be reconciled?

Answer reflection questions on the following page.

Reflections

Who do I need to go to be reconciled with today? List all who come to mind.

What actions or words need to be offered to the one I hurt in order to be reconciled?

Day 3

PRAYER OF LAMENT

Make allowance for each other's faults, and forgive anyone who offends you. Remember, the Lord forgave you, so you must forgive others.
Colossians 3:13

Today, try to think of groups or individuals who are not reconciled. This may be a person you have had a conflict with that ended your relationship. It could be a friend, family member, or coworker. Write a lament over the separation they, or you, are experiencing. Cry to God about the conflict that divides.

On the following page write your own Psalm of lament as your prayer for this person or group of people. You can insert your name or the names of others into the words you write to make it more personal. Then, allow this Psalm to be your cry, your prayer of lament to your Father.

My Prayer of Lament

Day 4

INTERCESSORY PRAYER

For Christ himself has brought peace to us. He united Jews and Gentiles into one people when, in his own body on the cross, he broke down the wall of hostility that separated us. He did this by ending the system of law with its commandments and regulations. He made peace between Jews and Gentiles by creating in himself one new people from the two groups. Together as one body, Christ reconciled both groups to God by means of his death on the cross, and our hostility toward each other was put to death.
Ephesians 2:14-16

Today continue with the prayer for the individuals or groups that you wrote about in your prayer of lament. Spend time today interceding, asking God to reconcile your relationship or the relationship of others you identified yesterday.

Begin with asking the Holy Spirit to show you how to pray for this person or group of people. Record what you receive.

If a scripture comes to mind about this person or people, use that as a way to pray. Record your intercessory prayer below.

Day 5

PRAYER OF THANKSGIVING

Yet now he has reconciled you to himself through the death of Christ in his physical body. As a result, he has brought you into his own presence, and you are holy and blameless as you stand before him without a single fault.
Colossians 1:22

Your faith journey began with being reconciled to God. Spend time in prayer today thanking God for that gift. Then list all the times in the past, you have experienced reconciliation with another person. After listing all the times you have reconciled, spend time thanking God for each of those relationships.

Write your prayer of thanksgiving for the ways the Holy Spirit has lead you to truth.

Day 6

LECTIO DIVINA

Read the following passages using the guide of Lectio Divina and record your thoughts. Read this passage slowly and carefully three times:

This means that anyone who belongs to Christ has become a new person. The old life is gone; a new life has begun! And all of this is a gift from God, who brought us back to himself through Christ. And God has given us this task of reconciling people to him. For God was in Christ, reconciling the world to himself, no longer counting people's sins against them. And he gave us this wonderful message of reconciliation
2 Corinthians 5:17-19

What one word or phrase sticks out as you read God's word?

Ask why God prompted you with this word or phrase.

Then continue on the following page.

Meditation
Think deeply on the spiritual reality within the text. Record your thoughts.

Contemplation
Resting in God's presence. Be still and sit in God's presence for a few moments.

Action
Go and do likewise. What has this passage, prayer and quiet time with God inspired you to go and do? List any actions you are prompted to take.

Day 7

CONCLUDING PRAYER

Wonderful Father, we see all the ways we disagree and stand apart within the body of Christ. We cry out to you to bring us together with a bond of unity.

For Christ himself has brought peace to us. He broke down the wall of hostility that separated us. Lead us further into unity.

Teach us how to love those who see the world differently. Teach us to learn from each other, to build each other up in spite of our differences.

For Christ himself has brought peace to us. He broke down the wall of hostility that separated us. Lead us further into unity.

Forgive us where we hurt others by our words and actions. Purify our hearts so our words become healing and unifying. Cleanse us from selfish ambitions that drive us apart from those we love.

For Christ himself has brought peace to us. He broke down the wall of hostility that separated us. Lead us further into unity.

Lead us into unity so the world sees something different in the body of Christ. Let us live the example of unity and love even when we disagree. Let us be a light to the world by our love for one another.

For Christ himself has brought peace to us. He broke down the wall of hostility that separated us. Lead us further into unity.

Week 6
JUSTICE

Justice

It appears that the call for justice emerges from three distinct sources: sacred truth, societal rules and laws, and from need and pain. From Genesis through Revelation, God addresses justice. Injustices committed were the crimes against individuals like Abel and Tamar. Injustices were committed against people groups, like the poor or the nation of Israel. We cannot escape the call for justice from the sacred truth of the Bible.

When justice emerges from societal law, individuals are also expected to adhere to that law and not challenge it. In the United States, we operate with a retributive justice model for our criminal justice system where punishment, when proportionally appropriate, is an acceptable response to crime and injustice.

What we must begin to realize is that justice may be prescribed by sacred truth and societal laws but the means to which justice is fulfilled is a very personal experience. There are hundreds of individuals sitting in prisons being punished by society's laws for the crimes they committed. And there are hundreds of their victims who still feel justice was not served. The pathway for the fulfillment of justice is often found in face to face conversations where truth is spoken, repentance offered, forgiveness granted, and reconciliation provided.

Let true justice prevail, so you may live and occupy the land that the Lord your God is giving you.
Deuteronomy 16:20

This week justice follows reconciliation for a reason. One goal of reconciliation should be justice in some form. Justice is a noun. Webster defines justice as, "the quality of being just; righteousness, equitableness, or moral rightness." Since it is not an action, it can easily become a concept or ideal that we need only to define.

It is important to remember that justice appears through three distinct paths: sacred truth, societal rules and laws, or from need and pain. These three distinctions help guide us as we seek to, facilitate reconciliation and ultimately justice. These distinctions will lead to the actions needed to bring about justice.

To do this it must be determined by those experiencing injustices which of the three paths to take to make things just: seek answers from scripture, seek legal actions, or seek justice through healing.

Day 1

CENTERING PRAYER

First and foremost, our desire is to seek and sit in the presence of our loving Father. Begin this week with centering prayer. Remember to allow yourself to focus on being present with the Triune God: the Father, Jesus, and the Holy Spirit. If you are new to centering prayer start with five minutes. You can always increase the time as you learn to remain in his presence.

After your prayer time journal any thoughts you have about the day or week ahead.

Day 2

READ AND REFLECT

Burdens Not Meant to Bear

Sandi's brother Alex died because of her. Yes, Marcos killed Alex in a drive-by shooting, but it was her fault. Sandi was fifteen when Alex died. His murder was the most devastating event in her life. She was dating a wanna-be gang member named Romero. Alex hated Romero and Sandi knew it. Secretly she liked that her brother was protective of her and wanter her to break up with her boyfriend. At the same time, she loved the fun they were having going out and cruising the town.

The night of Alex's murder, he and Sandi fought for the hundredth time. Alex confronted Romero earlier and threatened him, telling him to stay away from his sister. Standing in the room screaming at Alex, Sandi seethed with anger and disgust at her brother's high-and-mighty attitude. Not to mention, he took her last cigarette, and she had no money left to buy more.

"You can do better, Sandi!" Alex yelled as she stormed out of the room. Sandi didn't hear his truck start, but the pelting of hundreds of pebbles bouncing off the mobile home resounded his anger as he spun gravel speeding out of the carport. Her anger intensified that he chickened-out of the argument. Two hours later, her anger was gone, replaced by the jarring news of Alex's murder in, what appeared to be a gang-related, drive-by shooting. Immediately, she knew Romero was involved, and it was all her fault!

Ten years later, Sandi asked to meet with Marcos, the man in prison for murdering Alex. The jury convicted Marcos of the crime, but she was guilty, too.

Marcos was one of the few offenders I worked with as a mediator that took full responsibility for the crime from the moment we met. In fact, he was devastated to learn that Sandi felt responsible as well. Throughout the preparation, he agonized over the words he would say to ensure he didn't cause more harm to Sandi.

He explained that while he knew Romero and was at his apartment that day, there was never any discussion of Sandi or what happened with Alex. Marcos described himself as a stupid punk kid trying to impress other gang members by shooting someone in a drive-by. He was deeply ashamed of his cowardice, selfishness, and stupidity.

The dark rumbling clouds outside echoed the emotions of Sandi and Marcos the day they sat face to face in the prison visitation room. Words, grief, anger, sorrow, regret bounced around the room for hours and ended when Marcos extended his upturned arms across the cracked surface of the wooden picnic table between them.

"Tell me more. Tell me all the pain. Tell me all your anger. Please put them in my hands where they belong," whispered Marcos.

He moved his hands to his shoulders and continued, "because all your pain belongs to me. I am the guilty one."

Sandi wept. I saw the tense muscles along her jaw relax and eventually transform into a faint smile.

>She replied, "I don't know what life will be like, or what it will feel like to give up the guilt. But I will work on it. And I forgive you."

Marcos took the weight that belonged to him; the millstone of guilt transferred to its rightful owner. And yet, the miracle of forgiveness made the wretched adornment light as a feather.

Suffering wants to demand an accounting. But, we are not designed to carry great burdens. Who needs to say, "Place the pain on me, where it belongs." And who needs to say, "I forgive you." When both converge in a sacred moment, we will fulfill what the reckoning demands.

Answer reflection questions on the following page.

Reflections

Are there areas in your life, work, family, or community where you need to take responsibility to make things right and just? If so, list them here.

What steps do you need to take to bring justice to those situations?

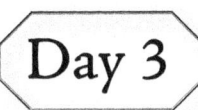

PRAYER OF LAMENT

Confuse them, Lord, and frustrate their plans, for I see violence and conflict in the city. Its walls are patrolled day and night against invaders, but the real danger is wickedness within the city.
Psalm 55:9-10

There are many different contexts in which injustice occurs. There are unjust systems that keep people in poverty. There are laws in our country that favor the powerful. There are so many issues where injustice is at the core; issues like immigration, gender equity, and LGBTQ are just a few. Choose an area of injustice that is close to your heart and write a prayer of lament for those impacted by the injustices surrounding that issue.

On the following page write your own Psalm of lament as your prayer for this sin. If you know of someone personally impacted by that injustice insert his or her name into the words you write to make it more personal. Then, allow this Psalm to be your cry, your prayer of lament to your Father.

My Prayer of Lament

Day 4

INTERCESSORY PRAYER

Listen to me, my people. Hear me, Israel, for my law will be proclaimed, and my justice will become a light to the nations. My mercy and justice are coming soon. My salvation is on the way. My strong arm will bring justice to the nations. All distant lands will look to me and wait in hope for my powerful arm.
Isaiah 51:4-5

Think back to your prayer of lament for the person or group of people currently experiencing injustice. Today spend time praying for them and interceding, asking that God give them strength as they endure the waiting for justice to arrive.

Begin with asking the Holy Spirit to show you how to pray.
Record what you receive.

If a scripture comes to mind about a person or group experiencing injustice, use that as a way to pray. Record your intercessory prayer below.

Day 5

PRAYER OF THANKSGIVING

This is what the Lord of Heaven's Armies says: Judge fairly, and show mercy and kindness to one another.
Zechariah 7:9

Today think of all the times you have seen justice prevail. Make a list of all the times that justice was done.

Record your prayers of thanksgiving for the faithfulness God showed in these situations.

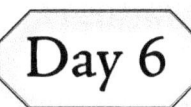

LECTIO DIVINA

Read the following passages using the guide of Lectio Divina and record your thoughts. Read this passage slowly and carefully three times:

Look at my Servant, whom I have chosen. He is my Beloved, who pleases me. I will put my Spirit upon him, and he will proclaim justice to the nations.
Matthew 12:18

What one word or phrase sticks out as you read God's word?

Ask why God prompted you with this word or phrase.

Then continue on the following page.

Meditation
Think deeply on the spiritual reality within the text. Record your thoughts.

Contemplation
Resting in God's presence. Be still and sit in God's presence for a few moments.

Action
Go and do likewise. What has this passage, prayer and quiet time with God inspired you to go and do? List any actions you are prompted to take.

Day 7

CONCLUDING PRAYER

Loving Father, open our eyes to see those around us suffering from injustice. Help us see the ones being hurt by unjust systems in our community, our church, our work, our families.

Lord of Mercy, hear our cries for our brothers and sisters. Let your Kingdom come.

Heavenly Father, give us courage to stand with the hurting. Do not allow us to turn our eyes from the injustice. Give us courage to fight to make things right.

Lord of Mercy, hear our cries for our brothers and sisters. Let your Kingdom come.

Wonderful Savior, give us compassion for those who exploit and seek to harm. Teach us to pray for the unjust as well as the just. Show us how to love those who hate and divide and hurt.

Lord of Mercy, hear our cries for our brothers and sisters. Let your Kingdom come.

Lord, you call us. You tell us what is good, what you require of us—to do what is right, to love mercy, and to walk humbly with you. Give us endurance as we journey to justice with you.

Lord of Mercy, hear our cries for our brothers and sisters. Let your Kingdom come.

Week 7
Love

Love

It is you
I see it is you
You are the horizon
You are the tide coming in
You are greener pastures
You are the open door
I see you coming
I hear your voice
You are my hope, on the other side of darkness
You are the light that pierces death
I see you coming
Come to me
Find me here
Touch my heart that I may awaken
That I may dance
That I may live
I see you coming
I hear your voice
Come to me
Find me here
That I may love again
Come

We know how much God loves us, and we have put our trust in his love. God is love, and all who live in love live in God, and God lives in them.
1 John 4:16

There is no shortage of conflict and strife in our current society. Every time we go to social media we are bombarded with images and stories of riots, protests, personal opinions, arguments, and polarization of almost every issue. Many followers of Christ are asking how to navigate such deep chasms of division. How do we begin the process of moving toward those we perceive as our enemies? How do we begin to make connections with others when we presume we have nothing in common?

Friends and colleagues express concern about saying too much, saying too little, or saying the wrong thing. The most common solution to that dilemma is silence. We are at a place in history where silence is no longer an option. We must diligently seek to bridge gaps and demonstrate the love of Christ we have personally experienced with others. The world is desperate to see the love of Christ in real tangible actions.

Day 1

CENTERING PRAYER

First and foremost, our desire is to seek and sit in the presence of our loving Father. Begin this week with centering prayer. Remember to allow yourself to focus on being present with the Triune God: the Father, Jesus, and the Holy Spirit. If you are new to centering prayer start with five minutes. You can always increase the time as you learn to remain in his presence.

After your prayer time journal any thoughts you have about the day or week ahead.

Day 2

READ AND REFLECT

This week we have a poem was written by the victim of a violent crime about shame and the love she found.

A Blanket of Shame

A blanket of shame covers me.
I was given this blanket many years ago.
It covers the sin.
It covers the nakedness.
It was so warm for so many years.
Under the blanket, I hid.
It never mattered that the threads used to weave the blanket were lies.
It never mattered that the dye for the shades of gray were my tears.
It only mattered that it covered my nakedness.
It only mattered that it covered the sin.
No one could see me under the blanket, and I liked it that way.
I could see them, but they could not, would not ever see me
And I liked it that way.

I went nowhere without my blanket.
I wore it constantly.
If I ever took it off my nakedness would show.
The sin would show.
There were times when I longed to shed the blanket
And twirl around and dance.
But I dare not.
They would see.
At first, it hid the nakedness,
It hid the sin.
But eventually, it covered my face.
I could not let them see my face.
They would look in my eyes and see.
I covered my face,
Until I had no face at all.

All my life I have wandered in the blanket of shame.
I have felt the threads of lies brush my cheeks.
I have heard the whispers of the lies rustle against my ears.
Reminding me of the sin.
Reminding me to hide.
Reminding me to hide my face, my eyes.

I let the blanket drop on occasions
When I thought it was safe.
But the gasps I heard when the sin showed,
When my nakedness showed,
Were too great to bear.
Oh, how I have longed for the day I could shed the blanket
And not hear the gasps, not see looks of unbelief on faces.
Oh, how I have longed for the day the blanket is shed, and I find
Open arms to comfort instead of eyes that shun.
The very same eyes that scream,
"Cover that sin, cover that nakedness, I don't want to look."

And so, I have grown accustomed to my blanket of shame.

You see me… you think.
You look at me and think you know me.
But what you see is not me.
You only see the blanket of shame that has become my face
Has become my eyes
Has become my life.
My Savior knows my shame,
He bore it on the cross.
He died to remove the blanket of shame that I wear.
Yet he knows I do not have the strength to let go.

He knows I am weak.
So, he secretly meets me beneath the lies.
He once again robes himself in the shame to come to me.
He gladly does this for me,
Because he loves me.
He sees the sin and does not shun.
He sees the nakedness and does not gasp.
He comforts me in secret places beneath a blanket of shame.
Because he knows I cannot bear to look into any more eyes that scream,
"Don't look. Cover up. That sin is ugly."
Maybe one day I will find the place where it is safe to shed.
Maybe I will meet the one that will see and not gasp.
Maybe I will find the place where my Savior and I can dance
And twirl and the threads of lies are gone
And only the soft breeze of the wind will whisper in my ears.
But, a blanket of shame covers me.
I was given this blanket many years ago.

You see me… you think.
You look at me and think you know me.
But what you see is not me.
You only see the blanket of shame that has become my face
Has become my eyes
Has become my life and it distorts my view of everything.

Answer reflection questions
on the following page.

Reflections

The author of this poem writes of how Christ secretly met her and was willing to step into her shame. Are you willing to invite Christ to step into your places of shame or weakness to experience his love in that place?

How can you better learn to enter into the suffering and pain of others?

Day 3

PRAYER OF LAMENT

Can those in the grave declare your unfailing love? Can they proclaim your faithfulness in the place of destruction? Can the darkness speak of your wonderful deeds? Can anyone in the land of forgetfulness talk about your righteousness? O Lord, I cry out to you. I will keep on pleading day by day. O Lord, why do you reject me? Why do you turn your face from me?
Psalm 88:11-14

Do you know individuals in your community that are longing to be loved? There are groups of people who are easily forgotten and pushed to the margins of society: the elderly, the disabled, the poor. Write a prayer of lament for those in your circle of life that feel lost and alone and unloved. Write the names of those you know who simply wish to experience love.

On the following page write your own Psalm of lament as your prayer for these individuals. You can insert the names of the individuals into the words you write to make it more personal. Then, allow this Psalm to be your cry, your prayer of lament to your Father.

My Prayer of Lament

Day 4

INTERCESSORY PRAYER

But I say, love your enemies! Pray for those who persecute you! In that way, you will be acting as true children of your Father in heaven. For he gives his sunlight to both the evil and the good, and he sends rain on the just and the unjust alike.
Matt 5:44-45

It is easy to pray for the hurting or lost or oppressed. But Christ has even greater expectations for us in that he tells us to pray for our enemies and those who persecute us. There are two options for prayer today:

1. Think of a time when you or someone you love was deeply hurt by another person. Then write your prayer for the one who caused the harm.
2. Think of a person or group that causes oppression or division in your community. Then write your prayer for that person or group.

Begin with asking the Holy Spirit to show you how to pray for that person. Record what you receive.

If a scripture comes to mind for those considered enemies, use that as a way to pray. Record your intercessory prayer below.

Day 5

PRAYER OF THANKSGIVING

Most important of all, continue to show deep love for each other, for love covers a multitude of sins.
1 Peter 4:8

Doing the work of a peacemaker has many challenges. You encounter the wounded and the ones who wound. The greatest gift you can give to those in conflict and division is love. We started this prayer journey looking at the sins that create the need for peacemaking. We will end this journey by thinking and praying to love deeply to cover those sins.

Make a list of the ways people have demonstrated love to you in the past year.

Record your prayers of thanksgiving for the people who loved you and the ways they showed their love.

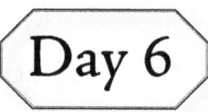

LECTIO DIVINA

Read the following passages using the guide of Lectio Divina and record your thoughts. Read this passage slowly and carefully three times:

Always be humble and gentle. Be patient with each other, making allowance for each other's faults because of your love.
Ephesians 4:2

What one word or phrase sticks out as you read God's word?

Ask why God prompted you with this word or phrase.

Then continue on the following page.

Meditation

Think deeply on the spiritual reality within the text. Record your thoughts.

Contemplation

Resting in God's presence. Be still and sit in God's presence for a few moments.

Action

Go and do likewise. What has this passage, prayer and quiet time with God inspired you to go and do? List any actions you are prompted to take.

Day 7

CONCLUDING PRAYER

Wonderful Father, thank you for forgiveness and the gift of new life in you. Your love is perfect, it never fails, and that nothing can separate us from your love. Help us love deeper.

Lord, fill us with the overflowing power of your love so we can make a difference in this world and bring honor to you, that we may show love as you have loved.

Jesus, you are the author of love. We know love because you loved us first. You love us in spite of our messiness and shortcomings. We thank you for this amazing love.

Lord, fill us with the overflowing power of your love so we can make a difference in this world and bring honor to you, that we may show love as you have loved.

Jesus, you also love us when we hurt others. You love us when we walk away from those in need. You love us when we refuse to listen and walk in your ways. Thank you for loving us this way.

Lord, fill us with the overflowing power of your love so we can make a difference in this world and bring honor to you, that we may show love as you have loved.

Jesus, we ask you to make us better lovers of one another. Give us a heart and love to offer to those in need. Teach us how to walk in you selfless, self-sacrificing love.

Lord, fill us with the overflowing power of your love so we can make a difference in this world and bring honor to you, that we may show love as you have loved.

FINAL THOUGHTS

FINAL THOUGHTS

FINAL THOUGHTS

www.ingramcontent.com/pod-product-compliance
Lightning Source LLC
Chambersburg PA
CBHW081457040426
42446CB00016B/3279